The Beginning

THE
BEGINNING

By: Danielle Osby

XULON PRESS

Xulon Press
2301 Lucien Way #415
Maitland, FL 32751
407.339.4217
www.xulonpress.com

Unless otherwise indicated, Scripture quotations taken from the King James Version (KJV) – *public domain.*

Paperback ISBN-13: 978-1-6628-4631-1
Ebook ISBN-13: 978-1-6628-4637-3

Table of Contents

The Before

*B*efore creation, God already knew what He was going to do and how it was all going to turn out. He calls Himself the Alpha and Omega in Revelation when He says, "I am the Alpha and Omega, the first and the last, the beginning and the end." Because of this, He knew the beginning from the end. He knew His creation before He spoke anything into existence. He knew what His creation would do before any of it came to be. Looking into what would be, across all of time, before a planet was placed, before the sun rose and set, before there was a light to separate the day from the night, He saw, and He knew, and He chose to create both in spite of what he saw. Nothing is a surprise to God because He has always been all knowing. He has always been all seeing. He has always been, and He always will be. It is difficult to understand that God has always existed but because He has always existed and was not created He alone is the ultimate Creator. He is called the Great I Am. He is known as the God Who Was, the God Who Is, and the God Who Will Be.

In the beginning of existence, there was only God the Father, Jesus the Son, and the Holy Spirit referred to as the Trinity, the Triune God, the Three in One. God had big dreams of creating a beautiful world for Himself where there would be true relationships for Him with others. A world where everyone would look to

Him and worship Him and Him alone. This worship would come from a desire to love and know Him. It would not be forced or manipulated. His love would awaken hearts who would in turn worship Him. This desire was not because God wanted to simply be adored. It was because God wanted to create to show His love. The relationship between the Creator and the Created is profound. It was birthed in the mind of God. Only the Creator knows what the Creation will become. The Creator is concerned with the design, every intricate detail, every piece, every part, every color and shape and unique feature. Only a Creator can envision the ultimate finish to the Creation. It becomes a relationship of caring and love and patience and thoughtfulness. And this is how it was when God, our Creator, created humanity.

He wanted us. He wanted humanity. He wanted a relationship. He wanted to give all that He had. He loved us first. He loved us before we came to be. He loved us with a love that would be everlasting. He loved us as only a Creator can love His creation.

He put everything together walking out each step of life with angels and humans with Himself as the foundation. The Bible says, "God's firm foundation stands, bearing this seal: 'The Lord know those who are His." He examines the hearts of humans. He knows everything's place. He leaves nothing out. God orchestrates every step. He desires everything to be perfect for His children. He desires for His children to experience His perfect love for them. He never intended for humans or angels to turn from His love. But because He is all knowing, He knew history would take a different path because of the desires of angels and humans. Yet still He continued to create in spite of everything He knew would take place and all the choices that would be made. He knew nothing would stop His will from being done. He knew He would still have everything the way He wanted in the end. God was truly pleased with everything He saw. Knowing every decision that would be made, every act of disobedience, every act of repentance, and every desire of every heart, He proceeded with the miracle of creation, and He called it good. This is a display of the heart of a loving Father. A Father who knows His children will make mistakes, have moments of rebellion, and at times promote disobedience, and yet continually loves His children in times of joy and sorrow, in times of loyalty and disobedience, in times of trust and betrayal. The love of God the Father was exhibited in His creation of humanity knowing full well what they would do.

The Heavens

" *In* the beginning, God created the heavens and the earth."
(Gen 1:1) The heavens are beautiful. They are made for
royalty. Heaven contains everything of beauty that can be imagined. Heaven contains kingdoms made for kings and queens, tem-
ples made for worship, and gardens filled with trees, flowers, fruits,
and vegetables. Most importantly, Heaven contain God's throne
because it is the place where He will dwell for eternity. His throne
is powerful. His throne is for Him and Him alone. His throne is
the representation of His authority. It is a reminder that He is the
Creator of all. His throne is where His presence dwells and where
His presence is there is fullness of joy and at His right hand are
pleasures forevermore. Flowing out of the throne is a river of water
of life that flows throughout Heaven. The heavens contain items
made of gold and silver meant to last for eternity. The best we
can do to describe Heaven in human terms is to describe the most
beautiful items we can think of, but nothing encompasses the true
beauty it contains. The Bible tells us, "No eye has not seen, nor
ear heard, nor the heart of man imagined, what God has prepared
for those who love Him."

"For in him all things were created: things in heaven and on
earth, visible and invisible, whether thrones or powers or rulers or
authorities; all things have been created through Him and for Him."

Nothing God does is small. His creation of the heavens and every-thing in them was perfect. He made sure the heavens had enough space for His next creation by building things just for them so that He could make sure all their needs were met. With the foundation in place, He knew He had established that He is the reason for everything so that they could look to Him with understanding that He is almighty. He was truly in love with His work, and He wanted them to be pleased as well. He made sure everything they could ever long for they would have.

The Angels

*A*fter creating heaven, God then focused on creating the angels who were to dwell in heaven for eternity. He created them one by one, then proceeded to dress them in royal garments. Once dressed, God looked proudly at them and gave them all names according to their purpose. There were Cherubim, winged angels whose purpose was to attend to God. There were Seraphim, angels of the highest order, symbols of purity. There were Archangels, angels with rule and authority who ruled over other angels. There were Living Creatures who looked part lion, part ox, part eagle, and part man who declared the holiness of God and led the other angels in worship. He created each angel different from each other. They all had their own unique purpose. He created male and female angels. He created some with wings others without. They were different sizes, some big and some small, and they all had different features. Some angels had many eyes, others had many wings, others were created with human features. The angels were beautiful with amazing voices, which they used to bring God glory continually from the time they were created.

God created the angels with unique purpose as well. He created angels to rejoice over repentance. He created angels to serve those who inherit salvation. He created angels to guard over humanity. He created angels to sing and rejoice. He created angels to be messengers. He created angels to war in the spirt realm. He created angels to proclaim the eternal Gospel to those who live on the earth. He created angels to sit at His right hand. He created angels to attend to Him. The Lord was pleased with all the angels He had created, He allowed them to dwell in heaven with Him.

At this time the angels knew no wrong. For the angels in the beginning had not yet been exposed to free will because they had just begun living. Without free will, there was no right from wrong. There was only the way the Creator created them to be. All of God's angels were perfectly made. Little did they know, God had bigger plans for them. They were truly experiencing the ultimate existence, worshipping the Lord, and working on His behalf. Nothing evil existed in the beginning. The angels worshipped God and filled Heaven with praise. They sang of His holiness and His worthiness. They sang of joy and rejoiced in His presence.

All the angels knew ultimate contentment. They had all that could be imagined. Dwelling in the most beautiful place ever created with the glory of God surrounding them, dressed in robes fit for royalty, all their needs were met. Everything was in order because God is a God of order. They worshiped Him and gave Him the highest praise. They would sing songs, dance, and praise the Lord. They made sure He was exalted above all. It was God's perfect plan. All their praises were given with pure hearts. God was pleased with His creation even though He knew some angels would soon turn and follow another.

The angels continued to fill the heavens with praise and worship and allowed everything they did to bring God the glory. They were truly experiencing the existence God intended for them. They were a unique and special part of God's creation and fulfilled a distinct purpose. They gave all of their devotion and attention to God and glorified Him. God continued with His plans. He was pleased with His creation. He captured the hearts of all the angels. They were content in His presence.

The angels were still in good hands with the Creator of the heavens and earth as He walked with them. At that time the angels only had two jobs, to worship the Lord and to serve Him. All day long they would praise the Lord. It was truly powerful. All the angels walking together in one accord surrounded by the joy of Heaven was truly amazing. They were blessed to be alive, and the Lord accepted their pure worship. To worship Him they would dance, sing, throw their hands in the air, shout out praises and fall down on their faces. They would cry, "Holy, holy, holy is the Lord God Almighty who was and is and is to come. Worthy is the Lamb, who was slain, to receive power and wealth and wisdom and strength and honor and glory and praise." They did all this with pure hearts. This captured God's heart. The angels were amazing creations giving God what He was due. At this time not one had evil motives until one angel caused a shift in the heavens and changed the atmosphere.

The Traitor

*H*is name was Lucifer. He was a little more unique than the rest. Lucifer started off just like the other angels. He praised the Lord and gave Him glory. He magnified the Lord with all he had and all he did. Some believe he was the leader of praise and worship. He found great joy in doing this until he began to notice how talented he was and how what he did made the other angels react. Lucifer was the most beautiful angel the Lord created. He was also very talented. He grabbed the attention of many angels. So, while doing this, Lucifer's popularity began to grow with the angels. So much so that they began to look to him instead of God. Mesmerized by what they were seeing, the other angels began giving Lucifer the highest praise. This praise belonged to God alone. By worshipping Lucifer in place of God they were committing the ultimate act of rebellion. The shifting of their praise from God to Lucifer only served to increase Lucifer's pride. God was not surprised by this turn of events. He already knew what was to come.

Lucifer saw the other angels respond to him and his pride caused him to desire to become God. He felt as though he could do what God did. He felt that he was on the same level as God. He continued doing what was evil in the Lord's sight by grabbing the attention of the angels and keeping the praise for himself. He continued desiring to be just like God and even greater. This desire drove him forward in his rebellion. This desire overtook his mind and produced every action of rebellion that was to come. The Bible says that Lucifer's heart became proud on account of his beauty, and he corrupted his wisdom because of his splendor. This means that Lucifer carried within him a wisdom that was from God and his pride allowed this godly wisdom to become corrupt. His splendor, created by God for God's glory became his downfall. He turned from worshipping the Creator to worshipping that which was created.

Many more angels turned from God and began to look to Lucifer. Lucifer had his way with the angels charming them and showing out. He used his wisdom and splendor, though corrupt, to lead them astray. He turned the angels away from the Lord with his evil motives and untrue promises that he would do far more for them then the Lord could do. This was a lie because Lucifer was not nor would he every be God. Nothing he could do would ever compare to the power of God.

God continued to be patient, and He allowed the angels to have a choice to serve Him or Lucifer. However, God would not allow Lucifer to keep the name He had given him. The Bible says that God calls all of His creation by name and that is because as the Creator, He creates everything unique and with His signature. Names mean something to God. God would demonstrate this throughout history as He named and renamed giants of the faith. God would not allow Lucifer to keep the name given to him at his creation. Because of Lucifer's prideful rebellion, God changed his name from Lucifer meaning "morning star" to Satan meaning "adversary". The heavenly relationship between God and Lucifer ended and the adversarial relationship between God and Satan began.

What can we learn from this turn of events? What can we learn about pride and rebellion and grace and God's love? What can we learn about obedience and choices? We do not know all the details of what happened from the point of Lucifer's rebellion to his removal from heaven and his reign as the Father of Lies with fellow fallen angels as his demonic followers. Are we different from the angels? Can we learn from the acts of Lucifer and the choices he made? What follows is an allegorical depiction of that time. It is a story that depicts what could have happened. It is a story that shows the love of God on full display. It is a story of the grace of God vs the rebellion of Satan. It is a story we can all learn from.

The Allegory

$\mathcal{T}$ime does not exist in the heavenly realm as it is known on earth, but Lucifer continued for *some time* with his rebellion. After three hundred earthly years of Lucifer's prideful display, when the last angel turned to worship Lucifer, God began to move. First, God gave Lucifer a chance to change his ways, a chance to let go of his pride, a chance to return to his first love. God told him the battle could end and eternal life could begin if he would just give up his fight for the throne, his prideful ways, and his disregard for the creative power of God and look back to Him. Lucifer's desire to be God was overwhelming and all consuming. Lead by his pride and the adoration he felt from other angels, he disregarded God's warnings. He did not hesitate to reject God's extension of grace because he believed he deserved greater. He did not understand that there is nothing greater than the grace of God.

In spite of the chance for change God presented, Lucifer had made his decision and so had God. God gathered all His chosen people who would walk the earth as believers and the angels together. Jesus was there among His people as a witness to what was about to take place. God the Father stood close to Jesus, covered by a cloud protecting His identity. Jesus stood close to the chosen people. Lucifer was among the angels. God began to move. God separated the rebellious angels from the devoted angels. He directed the rebellious angels over to one side and the devoted angels to the other side. He placed Lucifer in front of the rebellious angels. Then He began creating.

As He created, He spoke to the rebellious angels and told them about a placed called Hell. He told them they would no longer be called angels but would now be called demons. He was changing their names just as He did with Lucifer. He told them because they were no longer angels, they could not dwell in the heavens that were intended to be their eternal home. They must now dwell somewhere else. As He said this, He continued to create. The demons realized that what God was creating was their new home. They were filled with worry. Somehow, they knew that what God would create for them would not be anything like the heavens they had been in since they were created. Though they worshipped Satan, they were also fearful of him. They knew that they could not look to him for a new home. They instinctively knew that he could not create for them what God had created. What would this new home be like? Who would live there? How would Satan rule? Would there be a river? Would there be a throne? What would it be like to live outside of God's presence? The angels had made their choice and now they awaited their destination.

God proceeded to create. The place that He was creating was called Hell. It *appeared* extremely beautiful. The most beautiful thing they had ever seen. Had they been wrong to doubt? Would God create for them a new home even better than Heaven? While still creating, God exposed everyone's heart. He explained that the chosen people and Jesus had devoted, faithful hearts and that the devil and his demons had rebellious, faithless hearts. The exposure of the hearts did nothing to discourage the devil. In fact, it encouraged him. The devil, full of himself, began parading around and all the demons began to worship him. What started as willingly following who they thought would be the greatest angel ever had turned into a worship done out of fear. They knew questioning him would have consequences. Seeing this, God continued with the plan, and He began throwing things inside of Hell. The demons tried to look and see what God was throwing into Hell. They wanted to know what He was doing. They wanted to see because as much as they were devoted to Satan, they had a certain dread that was beginning to come over them for what was to come. They strained to see and make sense of what their eternal future would hold.

Then God began creating angels to replace the angels that sided with the devil. The creative power of God was always at work. Pride and rebellion could not stop it. At this time, three demons began to talk amongst themselves. That feeling of dread they were experiencing began to overtake them. They knew they had made the wrong choice. They knew that God's presence is where they belonged. They knew that heaven was their home, so they ran back to God, asking to turn back to Him and worship Him alone. God allowed them to become angels again because He is a God of compassion. He let the demons and the devil know there was still time because they had not yet been cast away. They could still return to Him as the three angels did. His extension of grace was given again. The gift of His grace remained.

Then He continued creating the final destination for the devil and his demons. Hell was very dark inside so they couldn't see what was on the inside although the outside appeared very beautiful. God took Hell and knocked it down out of heaven. Then He knocked down all the demons. After that, He kicked Satan out of heaven into Hell along with the demons. The Bible says that Satan's fall from heaven to Hell was so swift and so powerful that he fell like lightning. The morning star was no more. God joined them as He had more to show them and more to tell them.

It may be hard to believe but during this time God was still moving forward with His plan. He was still creating. He spoke light into existence. He used the light to separate the darkness. He separated the waters putting water on the earth. He created the sky above the waters. He moved the waters on the earth and set boundaries for them creating dry land. On the dry land he created seed bearing fruit and vegetation. He then created the sun and the moon to light the earth both day and night. He looked to the seas and spoke into being living creatures so that the waters were teeming with life. He looked to the sky and spoke into being living creatures so that the air was teeming with life. He looked to the land and spoke into being living creatures so that the land was teeming with life. Life! It was the most important part of God's creation thus far. He looked at all of it and saw that it was good because He is good.

Then the pinnacle of God's creation began. The purpose and destiny and fulfillment of this part of creation filled the heavens. "So, God created mankind in his own image, in the image of God he created them; male and female he created them." This was the first of God's creations made in His image. The angels were beautiful and unique, created by God's power. The light, the water, the sea creatures, the sun, the moon, the flowers and vegetation, the crawling and flying creatures, were all beautiful. They all existed to give God glory. They were all created to show His power and prove His existence. But nothing, nothing in all of creation compared to the creation of humanity. Nothing compared to being created in the image of God.

God created man from the dust of the ground. This may not seem like a glorious creation. Taking dust from the ground to perform the pinnacle of creation does not seem worthy of the intricacy with which the human body and mind were created. The synapses of nerves, the connection of tendons to bone, the arteries and veins, the optic nerve, skin cells stretched over a skeleton of perfectly connected bones and ligaments tying muscle in place, the larynx and vocal chords working in unison for voice and song, the shape of the ear with perfectly in sync stirrup, anvil, and hammer bones producing the ability to hear, the olfactory system to take in the sweet scent of the fruit and the flowers, all of this was masterful. It seemed too masterful to have been created from dust, but God does not waste, and God does not look at dust as something left over or not worthy of being used. He gathered dust and He created His masterpiece in His image. Creating from the dust as He did, there would be no option to deny the creative power of God. There would be no other explanation for something so amazing and unique and beautiful. It could not have been created by chance. And then He did what He had not done with animals or the birds or the sea creatures. He breathed the breath of life into man. The breath of God dwells within every human being, and this is what produced the masterpiece. This is what made the creation of humanity the pinnacle of God's creation. This was the Master's special touch. Man was created identical to God in appearance and within man dwelled the characteristics of God: love, compassion, peace, and kindness.

There came a point in creation when that man, Adam, did not want to be alone. He had the creatures of the earth as his companions, but he desired another human to fellowship with. The desire for fellowship was created by God in Adam and every human since has within them the desire to fellowship with others and with God. God, not desiring for man to be alone caused Adam to fall into a deep sleep. He took Adam's rib and from the rib, he created a woman. Man may have been created identical to God in appearance, but there were secrets hidden in the creation of the woman's body.

When someone becomes a believer in Jesus, The Holy Spirit enters the body. The believer carries the Holy Spirit within them just like a mother carries a baby on the inside of her. They both are considered a new life. With the Holy Spirit the old life has passed away and new life has begun, it's spiritual. When bad things are put into the body it has the potential to harm or kill the baby in the womb. The same is true if someone puts bad things in the body or allows evil ways to come in and dictate how to live. It becomes harmful physically and spiritually. The only thing that is going to happen is a spiritual death. Jesus' blood washes away sin. Just like a woman's body purifies itself with blood. The Holy Spirit speaks for us in groanings like a woman is childbirth. These hidden gems within the creation of the woman's body were meant to show the creative power of God. Everything about the creation of man and woman was intended to point to God. God was creating all of this while Satan rebelled. Hell was never intended for humanity. It was intended for Satan and his demons.

In Hell, Satan looked around and was amazed. Hell was beautiful inside. It had everything Satan and his demons could ever ask for. Satan felt his ego and rose up again because he believed that God was creating something special for him. He believed his rebellion had won and this was part of his reward. The audacity of Satan was in full effect. To know that he was created to give God glory and then to openly rebel against Him convincing many angels to do the same and then to believe that God would reward him by creating something special for him shows the depth of his pride. The thing about pride is that with it comes deception. Those with pride in their hearts are deceiving themselves. Their pride begins to be the filter through which they see and interpret everything else. Pride leads to an ego-centric, selfish life. Pride takes down anyone in its path. Pride gives up the greatest of gifts thinking that there will always be more. This was the pride that consumed Satan and dictated his prideful actions.

In contrast to Satan's pride, was God's compassion and grace. God let them know there was still time to turn back to Him. He explained that there was still time to put aside their prideful ways and rebellious spirits. There was still a way to return to the perfection and beauty of heaven and the assignments they had been created to fulfill. The devil was moved, he was stirred but not enough to give in to God's grace. He continued in his ways and ignored what God had to say because he still wanted to be God. That is another thing about pride, the prideful heart believes that it can accomplish the impossible without God's help. To become God would require an act of God but Satan was just arrogant enough to think it might just happen through his power alone.

Having provided an opportunity for the demons and Satan to turn back to Him, God was ready to move forward with His plan. The power of God swept over them, and the devil and his demons began to tremble. In spite of their new found home and Satan's display of so called authority, the power of God was something that could not be thwarted or ignored. It could not be stopped. It could not be overcome. It was all consuming and it belonged to God alone. God's power was the power Satan sought after and the power he believed he would one day have. How foolish of Satan to believe he would ever be worthy of the power of God. How foolish of Satan to believe that he could stand in the presence of the power of God with no consequence.

God explained to them that they were wearing royal garments. The royal garments they were wearing were intended for heaven. They were heavenly garments. They were gifts from God given to them to wear as they worshipped around His throne. Heaven was a place of royalty. He told them since they no longer resided in Heaven and no longer fulfilled their heavenly duties, they needed to take the garments off.

Though many demons were trembling and fearful, their fear of Satan overtook their fear of God and only two demons heeded the words God spoke. They remembered the joy of Heaven. They remembered the purpose and the uniqueness of their royal garments. They remembered the love of God and the joy of His presence. They remembered the throne and the peace that came with being with their Creator and they ran back to God to become angels again. God accepted them and their royal garments remained. Their fear immediately subsided, and the joy of God's presence surrounded them. Peace replaced fear the instant they were in God's presence.

The remaining demons proceeded with taking off their garments and putting on the dark colored clothing that was there for them to wear. This clothing felt nothing like the royal garments they had removed. The royal garments had felt light and freeing. In fact, now that they had been removed, the demons realized they hadn't felt like garments at all. They had felt like part of them. Like what flowed in Heaven, the peace and joy and contentment, had flowed through the garments themselves. The new clothing felt heavy, and the darkness of the cloth seemed to rise up and become all encompassing. They watched the devil to see how he would react to his new garments. He was their leader and perhaps if he felt the heaviness, he would lead them back. They watched as the devil put on the clothes. He spun and admired his new clothes. He seemed to have no regard for the royal garments now laying at his feet. The devil also put on a hat and feeling good about himself he began to parade around. The demons saw that their leader seemed free. He seemed not only content in his new clothes, but joyful so again they began to worship him hoping worshipping him would bring the same freedom they felt when they worshipped God. They could not have been further from the truth for as they worshipped, the opposite of freedom came upon them, captivity. The Bible says, "For God did not spare angels when they sinned but cast them into hell and committed them to chains of gloomy darkness to be kept until the judgment. And the angels did not stay within their own position of authority, but left their proper dwelling, and He has kept them in eternal chains."

Then the devil began to look around at everything God had placed in Hell, and he felt insulted. He could do better. He didn't want God to get the glory for creating something else. He didn't want his demons to think that God had any part in their new home. As he looked around, he saw some large bags. He grabbed the bags and began placing everything in Hell inside the bags because he didn't want anything that reminded him of God to be there. The demons saw and began to help fill the bags as well. The devil expected this but what he did not expect was to see that God had also begun to help. Again, in his prideful arrogance, Satan thought that he has won. He thought that God has surrendered. What a fool! How deceived he was by his own thoughts! The Father of Lies was lying to himself because if he had faced the truth, he would have known that he would never win. God's authority would remain from everlasting to everlasting.

After finishing the clearing out of Hell, God told the devil and his demons there was still time. There was still time to return to Him and their heavenly home. There was still time to remove their heavy, dark, all-consuming garments for their original royal robes, if they would just turn back to him. But still, they did not return. Still, they chose to remain outside of their purpose. Still, they chose to follow the devil who never did anything for them, who never provided for them or cared for them or created for them. Still, they decided that living in rebellion was better than living in God's presence. Still, they rejected God's extension of grace. Since Hell was now empty of all things, God and the devil took a seat on the floor. How strange it was for the demons to see this. Heaven had been filled with the throne of God and beautiful structures, rivers of living water, and streets of gold. Now they stood in a place of vast nothingness surrounded by an emptiness that seemed to never end and God was seated not on a throne but in the midst of the nothingness. Then God looked at the devil and told him that He had created man and woman. The devil immediately got up and left.

The devil went to the woman with a plan to deceive her. Now was his chance to prove he deserved the throne. It was his chance to prove he deserved the adoration coming from his demons. It was his turn to show that he had a level of power that could be exerted over humanity. He took the form of a serpent and set out to discredit God. If the woman could doubt God's love, His intentions, and His words she could easily be deceived. Doubt and lack of trust were key ingredients to turning the woman's attention from God to him. The key was to take the words God had said and twist them slightly, to add just a few extra words and bring about confusion, doubt, and lack of trust. The devil did just as he planned.

He found the woman at the tree, and he asked her, "Did God really say, 'You must not eat from any tree in the garden?'" At first the woman responded thoughtfully. She recalled what God actually said and replied to Satan, "We may eat from the trees in the garden, but God did say 'You must not eat fruit from the tree that is in the middle of the garden, and you must not touch it, or you will die.'" Satan immediately responded by discrediting God's words. He planted a seed in the woman's mind that God had lied to her. He said, "You will not certainly die." Now, God had told the woman and the man that if they ate from that tree they would die. Satan had no right and no authority to lie about what God had said. The woman had no reason to doubt what God had said. From the moment of her creation, God had only given good gifts. He had provided the garden in its abundance. He has walked with her and the man. He had created for them a companionship with each other and with Him. The woman had no reason not to trust her Creator as He has always proven Himself to be a loving, caring, protective Father, but Satan lied, and the woman doubted. The woman allowed the seed of doubt he planted in her mind to grow.

Satan continued, "God knows that when you eat from it your eyes will be opened, and you will be like God, knowing good and evil." In saying this, Satan took another step in his discrediting of God. Not only did he tell the woman that God lied, but he also now told her that the reason God lied was because he didn't want the man and the woman to be like Him. Satan left out the fact that they were already made in God's image. The truth was, God made that boundary because He loved them and cared for them and wanted them to walk with Him in the garden without a care or worry. He didn't want them to be exposed to evil. He didn't want them to be in danger. He didn't want them to know sin and destruction and lies and deception and consequences. He wanted to protect them. He wanted them to always know the peace of garden.

Just as pride had risen in Satan's heart causing him to rebel against God, a type of pride rose up in the heart of the woman. She looked at the fruit and saw that it was pleasing to the eye and good for food and desirable for wisdom and she gave in and disobeyed God. Her pride allowed her to think that she knew better than God, that God's instructions to her did not matter. The man, who was with her, gave in as well and disobeyed. He ate the fruit. He too allowed his pride to dismiss the voice of God. This set-in motion a series of events that would change the world. Future people would look back and believe they would have done different. They would accuse both the man and the woman of being easily deceived. Yet, their decision was of their flesh. The decision to listen to Satan was a decision to silence the voice of God. All of humanity has struggled since with pride and the dismissal of God's voice.

Once the deception was complete, Satan came back to Hell and paraded around. The demons went crazy in their celebration of the devil's accomplishment as he told them what he had said and how easily he had deceived them. He explained how quickly both the woman and the man turned from God's words to his own and the demons blindly worshipped him. Before God created the heavens, before He created the angels, before he created man and woman, He knew this would happen. He saw it yet knew that His love would overcome. Their disobedience was painful. He loved the man and woman, but He had to speak to them and give them the predetermined consequences for their disobedience.

The man and woman, realizing that they had done wrong, hid in the garden hoping God would not find them, but then they heard the sound of God walking in the garden. They tried to hide, but they could not hide from God. His love would not allow them to. His love would never allow a human to hide from Him. He would make always make himself known. God called to the man, "Where are you?"

Now, God knew where the man was because He is all knowing. Yet God asked the man where he was because He wanted the man to come to Him and acknowledge Him. He wanted the man and woman to come to him and admit their disobedience. The man replied, "I heard you in the garden, and I was afraid because I was naked, so I hid." God asked how they knew they were naked. There had been no shame in being naked but now the shame they felt for their sin overcame them and they noticed their physical nakedness. This was man's opportunity to tell God the truth. This was man's opportunity to accept responsibility for the choices that were made, to ask God for his grace, but instead the blame game began.

The man replied, "The woman you put here with me, she gave me some fruit from the tree, and I ate it." The woman said, "The serpent deceived me, and I ate." The man blamed the woman. The woman blamed the serpent, and no one acknowledged what truly happened. This is how pride works. Pride never acknowledges wrongdoing. Pride always blames and always provides excuses. Pride says it is always someone else's fault at all costs. God then handed out the penalty for sin. He cursed the serpent itself and its future offspring to slither on the ground. To the woman he gave pain in childbirth and friction in the relationship of husband and wife. To the man he gave the curse of working to get food. To the ground he cursed the way it would produce. It would no longer be the ease of the garden.

God's Rest

*W*hen the devil left, God rested. After all He had done and been through with His creation, He decided to take a break from everything and get some rest. Now, it was not known how long He rested, only that He did. God rested even though he did not need to rest. God rested not because He could become tired. God never sleeps nor slumbers. God rested to set an example for humanity. God knew that He would be encouraging His people to take a day of rest set aside for Him. A day where they would gather together and focus on Him and His goodness. By resting, God set a pattern for His people. This was just another symbol of His love.

One adversary: Satan, one woman: Eve, one man: Adam, one choice: Sin and the consequences had a ripple effect throughout all of creation. But hidden in the curses was a gem. God said that the offspring of Eve would crush Satan. This offspring that He spoke of would be Jesus, His son sent to earth in human form to be born of the virgin Mary, a descendent of Eve. Jesus, the offspring, would come to take away the sins of the world. He would come to crush the head of Satan. In God's plan He had already placed an answer to the disobedience and rebellion that would take place. In the curse, God provided hope. This is another symbol of His great love and an extension of His grace.

God returned after being with the man and woman When the devil saw God, his pride arose within him once again and he began to create. His pride allowed him only to create that which is evil and rebellious. Being the Father of Lies, the devil could only create what was void of truth and goodness. He could only create that which would do his evil bidding. God looked at him and said, "You are creating demons." Then the devil stopped. Suddenly he could no longer move. He was overwhelmed and God asked him, "Can you feel that?" The devil and his demons tried to breathe but could not. It was as if all the air was removed from the room. They gasped and struggled and then there was silence.

In the silence, they heard their own heartbeats. Their heartbeats sped up and then slowed down until they completely stopped. They died. The peace and joy for which they were created ceased. The purpose for them to fulfill ended. The access to God and Heaven was no longer theirs. They became the living dead. Then God told the devil that because he deceived the woman and caused the man to fall, he was going to be punished. The man and woman had received their punishment and the devil must receive his for the role he played in their Fall.

God began by knocking Hell on its belly. The devil saw the tilt, he heard Hell fall but being ever filled with pride he smirked and said, "I'm still upright." God continued by knocking the devil on his belly and told him he would forever be under man's feet and that the seed of the woman would crush his head. God told him that he would be defeated by His Son. He told him that the defeat would be born out of love, not pride. This enraged the devil. He was incensed at the thought that he would be under the feet of men and that love would triumph. He was powerful and had just destroyed God's plan for the man and woman with his prideful ways. Surely, he would defeat all of God's created beings. What the devil didn't know was that this was just the beginning of his consequences.

God explained that the woman's seed, Jesus, would come and destroy the works of the devil. He then looked at the devil and said, "You are a murderer, you do not hold to the truth, and there is no truth in you. When you lie you speak your native language for you are a liar and the father of lies. You will come to steal and kill and destroy but my son Jesus will come to give life and life abundantly. My followers will resist you and when they do, you will flee. My Son will crush you under His feet. At the proper time you will be seized and bound with a great chain for 1,000 years, thrown into the Abyss, locked in, and sealed up. You will attempt to throw fiery darts at my followers, but they will stand against you and your flaming arrows will be extinguished. You will attempt to accuse those who follow Me, but your voice will be silenced."

Satan's pride would not win in the end. The victory he felt when returning from deceiving the man and woman would not last forever. As God was leaving Hell, He looked at the devil and his demons and said, "Apart from Me, you can do nothing."

Men and women then began to fill the earth. They were fruitful and they multiplied. When the first man who did not accept God died and went to Hell, the devil saw him and told him to worship him. The devil, having originally been created for worship, assumed this was the first thing he should ask of the man. However, the man did not understand how to worship because he had not served God. True worship is born out of a love for God and His presence but since the man had rejected God, he had never truly worshipped. Being ignorant of how to worship, he did not follow the devil's command and did not worship him. The man just looked up and cried out to the Lord because he felt the separation from his Creator.

The Lord spoke to the man and said, "I never knew you." The devil became very angry that the man was not paying him any attention. After everything, creation still looked to God. They still cried out to Him even from the devil's home. The devil was enraged. The devil was not used to being ignored. The devil wanted the attention and praise of the man. But the man was more interested in crying out to the Lord. The devil's rage turned to violence, and he went and got something sharp. If the man would not willingly worship him, he would use force. He returned to the man, took the sharp tool, and dug the man's eyes out so the man could no longer look up. The devil thought by removing his eyes, he could change his heart. The devil did not understand that the man was not interested in physically seeing God, he wanted to be with Him.

The devil told the man to worship him, but the man still wouldn't or maybe it was that he couldn't. The man was consumed with dread and regret. He was only filled with fear and an unquenchable desire to be with God. Though in his life he had rejected God, in his death he knew he had made the wrong choice. He cried out to God in anguish and desperation. This only increased the devil's rage and anger. His prideful mind could not withstand that the man would not worship him and that the man would dare cry out to God. What began as rage and turned to violence now evolved into torture. The devil began to torture the man. That is how torture began in Hell. Every person that entered Hell after the first man received the same torturous treatment. They must endure the climate, the lack of air, separation from God, and torture for eternity. The process never ends. It is all led by Satan's all-consuming pride.

The Lesson

$\mathcal{G}$od says that a good tree cannot produce bad fruit. If this is true, how did God who is good, produce the devil? The devil separated himself from God like fruit from a tree. When fruit is separated from the tree it no longer has the life-giving support and nutrients it needs and the only thing that can happen is for the fruit to die. See, a good tree will produce good fruit but once that fruit is removed from the tree it will turn bad and die. It is what happens to us, when we die. Our bodies decay because our bodies are no longer connected to life-giving support and nutrients. This is what happened spiritually to the angels that turned from God. They separated themselves from that which gave them life and the only thing that could happen was spiritual death. Their bodies no longer displayed the glory of God the Creator. They no longer were surrounded by life-giving peace and joy but instead they looked like corpses. They were hollow shells having lost what made them a royal part of God's Heavenly community. They were separated from their purpose.

The same is true of us. When we separate ourselves from God through sin, we too die spiritually and when our bodies die, we will be separated from God as well. But when we turn from sin, accept God into our lives, and walk in obedience we gain life. We begin developing the characteristics of the good tree because we

31

are grafted into the vine therefore, we gain our eternal bodies. The Bible says, "I (God) am the vine; you are the branches. If a man remains in me and I in him, he will bear much fruit; apart from me you can do nothing." From that point on, our foundation is secure in God.

God wants us to know He is always there for us no matter what decision we make. Just like He was for the devil. He doesn't even leave those who reject Him and do not believe in Him until they die. These individuals experience death without eternal life with God. He continually makes Himself known to humanity through creation, through circumstances, through the Word of God, through other people, through dreams, and through miracles. He is not willing that any should perish. His love for us is extravagant. He loves us in spite of our sin and turning. His mercy and grace are available to us. He desires for us to turn to Him and live our lives in relationship with Him. If we choose this life, a life dedicated to God, our lives just continue after death. We will look upon our Savior's face in eternity.

Choosing to walk with God is not always easy. It takes a lot of discipline. The more we grow in our relationship with God, the more we are willing and able to live our lives in the light of His love. Fighting our flesh is a daily battle. We must crucify our flesh daily and surrender to the Holy Spirit. Because it can be challenging, it helps to outline and understand what it takes. It starts with an idea, which becomes a plan. The plan requires preparation. To be prepared you have to gather the tools that are needed. Then you begin building your foundation and creating stronger and stronger levels. Once a strong foundation is laid, maintaining that foundation is crucial and takes discipline. God is there throughout the whole journey. He never leaves us nor forsakes us. God is love.

Idea: *Understanding God is Real (Believing in Jesus).* For many the question of "how do you know God exists" is of crucial importance. Pages can be filled with evidence that there was an Intelligent Designer of the Universe and all that is in it. The fact that order never comes out of chaos proves an orderly Creator exists. The fact that design exists in everything from an ant to Mount Kilimanjaro proves there is a creative Creator. The fact that the desire in the human mind for companionship and love exists proves there is a loving Creator. The fact that there is a moral code proves there is a just Creator. The proof of God is everywhere but it is also a matter of faith. The Bible says if we seek Him, we will find Him. He is ready and available. It may seem strange to begin a conversation with Someone you cannot see but by simply beginning a conversation, He will begin to reveal Himself.

Plan: *Changing your life and living for God*. Living a life for God seems difficult and for some even boring if you do not understand who He is. But when you believe God exists and put your faith in Him and get to know Him, the more your heart and mind turn towards Him, and your life is directed by Him. Putting God first regardless of circumstance and making a point to never let go of that first love keeps you on track. Though giving up some parts of your "old" life may be difficult, you will begin to feel peace and joy that you did not feel when living a life outside of God.

Preparation: *Developing a relationship with God and reading the Bible*. As you turn towards Him a strong relationship develops. As you read the Bible it is no longer filled with stories or words you don't understand. It becomes a way that God Himself speaks to you and reveals Himself to you. The more you get the Word inside of your temple the more you grow. That's one thing no one can take away from you. The Bible says that we hide God's Word in our hearts so we will not sin against Him. We are to equip ourselves with our minds directed on Him and His Word all day. As we meditate on the Word it will begin to show us how to live. "The Word of God is living and active, sharper than any two-edged sword, it penetrates even to divide soul and spirit, joints and marrow; it judges the thoughts and attitudes of the heart."

Tools needed: *God's Word inside of you and Fellowship with Believers*. As you read His word, it makes its way into your heart and your mind. It transforms how you think and how you live. The things that once seemed normal to you, no longer do. The supernatural understanding of life begins to be established in your life. Once you have the Word inside of you and you're meditating on Him all day then you can operate out of pure love. You can also hear from God more clearly so that you can walk in obedience. The tool of fellowship is a much needed, highly underrated tool. God Himself is a God of fellowship, connection, and relationship. He desires us to be in relationship with each other as believers. The Bible says, "Behold how good and how pleasant it is when brothers live together in unity." God is clear that He desires for us to fellowship. The Book of Hebrews says, "Let us not neglect meeting together, as some people do, but encourage one another, especially now that the day of His return is drawing near." The tool of fellowship will help us grow on our journey with God.

Beginning Foundation: *God is at the center of everything you do*. God becomes the center of your life not because you are religious or forced to have Him at the center but because it is your desire to be with God in every area of your life. God begins to reveal things to you and speak to you in supernatural ways. You begin to experience miracles and speak to other people through the lens of God's love. God is the chief cornerstone of our lives. The purpose of a cornerstone is to be the first stone laid for a structure and it becomes the reference for all other stones. When we build our life on The Chief Cornerstone, He becomes the reference point for all other areas of our lives. Ephesians says, "Now, therefore, you are no longer strangers and foreigners, but fellow citizens with the saints and members of the household of God, having been built on the foundation of the apostles and prophets, Jesus Christ being the Chief Cornerstone, in whom the whole building, being fitted together, grows into a holy temple of the Lord, in whom you also are being built together for a dwelling place of God in the Spirit."

Creation: *Operating effectively*. When this happens, you are living an abundant life. You are living life to the fullest. You are operating effectively, the way God created you to operate. God is your foundation, and you are walking according to His Word and His will for your life. This is where you begin to minister to others. This is when you can see and sense and feel what others are going through and the compassion of God can operate through you. This is when the Holy Spirit is in control. His voice leads and guides and encourages and corrects and speaks. God's voice is the loudest and strongest voice in your life. When He speaks you obey, and you operate for His glory and His honor.

Maintaining Discipline. *Discipline becomes a part of your daily life*. This is not because you have done wrong but because your heart's true desire is to submit itself to God and live your life in the light of His love. This is where discipline becomes not something that hurts so much as something to correct and direct. It doesn't mean that you are always joyful about the discipline that comes or glad to be corrected. It means that you understand the purpose of discipline and the intention of the Father when He disciplines. It is done out of love. Maintaining a long genuine relationship with God is not the easiest thing to do. Oftentimes this is because we make Him this far away God who is untouchable. Or we face a trial, and the outcome is not what we wanted or what we prayed for, and we begin to question Him and doubt the truth of His Word. But here is where the strong foundation comes in. Jesus talks about this in Matthew when He says, "Therefore everyone who hears these words of mine and puts them into practice is like a wise man who built his house on the rock. The rain came down, the streams rose, and the winds blew and beat against that house; yet it did not fall, because it had its foundation on the rock. But everyone who hears these words of mine and does not put them into practice is like a foolish man who built his house on sand. The rain came down, the streams rose, and the winds blew and beat against that house, and it fell with a great crash." God is our rock and our firm foundation. The truth is He's walking with us and always has been.

Children of God need to understand that there is no need to fear the devil because he is not omnipresent. There's just one of him. Once we become children of God, the devil and his demons become our enemies. His prideful ways continue. His rage continues. He cannot understand, even after thousands of years, why humans would choose to worship God. His torment of those who have died after rejecting God shows that he does not desire to lead out of love or care. He simply desires humans to reject God. He is called the Father of Lies, the Deceiver of the Brethren, and the Adversary. His only objective is to get followers of God to turn on God and turn towards him, just as he did. This is a lot to take in but, there is no reason to fear.

The spirit realm, where the spiritual battles take place, is the unknown and we can't see it, but it is truly nothing to fear. The devil is just a fallen angel. The reason God created angels was to fill Heaven with praise and to have loyal beings who would be messengers sent to serve those who inherit salvation. Angels are given specific tasks and assignments. These tasks and assignments are to accomplish God's will and to draw humanity towards Him. The devil and his demons twisted everything and instead of helping humans they started hurting them by getting in their heads.

There's really nothing special about the devil and his demons. The devil does not have the power to affect our physical bodies without God allowing it. If God does allow it, it would be considered a test from God to build us up in our faith like we read about in the book of Job. This helps us to understand that God is in control. The devil is not. A lot of times, we mistake trials that we are going through thinking that it is the enemy when it is really one of God's tests. God is truly trying to make us stronger so we can then go and help strengthen others.

The devil and his demons try to gain power through our fear. Impartation of fear, doubt, anxiety, depression, and causing us to question the promises of God are all tactics used by the devil. When we fear him or other circumstances of life, we give him power over us. Once fear is established, he continues to pursue us. He makes us think he is over everything bad that happens to us. When he does this, we think about him more than we think about God, and this magnifies him. When he is magnified, he gains power. We have given him power. He does not possess ultimate power alone. He needs us to allow our fear to give him access and access is power. We must fight back by gaining strength in our minds. That strength comes from the power of God and the Word of God. When we operate in God's strength, we defeat the tactics of the devil.

The Bible tells us a well thought out way to defeat the enemy. "Finally, be strong in the Lord and in his mighty power. Put on the full armor of God, so that you can take your stand against the devil's schemes. For our struggle is not against flesh and blood, but against the rulers, against the authorities, against the powers of this dark world and against the spiritual forces of evil in the heavenly realms. Therefore, put on the full armor of the God so that when the day of evil comes, you may be able to stand your ground, and after you have done everything, to stand. Stand firm then, with the belt of truth buckled around your waist, with the breastplate of righteousness in place, and with your feet fitted with the readiness that comes from the gospel of peace. In addition to all this, take up the shield of faith, with which you can extinguish all the flaming arrows of the evil one. Take the helmet of salvation and the sword of the Spirit, which is the word of God. And pray in the Spirit on all occasions with all kinds of prayers and requests."

Jesus, Himself never wasted time by preparing us for the devil and his demon. Yes, He did cast them out, but He didn't dwell on them. I believe it's because the biggest enemy is not the devil. It lies in human excuses {which we all know stems from choice}. Had Adam admitted his wrongdoing in the garden, I believe the punishment would not have been as harsh.

Children of God should fear the Lord and magnify Him. This is not a fear that comes with dread. This is a fear that comes out of reverence and respect. The fear of the Lord is the beginning of living a wisdom filled life. The fear of the Lord brings joy and contentment and builds relationships. As God's followers focus on Him, fear Him, and magnify Him, the enemy's hand and presence will end up getting weaker and weaker as time goes by. The effects will no longer be great. The devil and his demons will notice that nothing they do in your life works so they will keep giving up and fleeing. Resist the devil and love your enemy and always remember to put God first.

The devil did not win at The Beginning when he rebelled against God. He did not win when he deceived the man and the woman. He did not win when his followers were changed from angels to demons. He did not win when Hell became occupied. The devil did not win, and he will never win. God is in control and the devil knows his fate is to be thrown into the Abyss. He knows that God will reign for eternity. He may try to do all he can to change his fate, but his fate was written before he existed.

Important Standouts:

$\mathcal{E}$verything in the beginning was good. The angels knew no wrong. Everything was perfect so the concept of anything going wrong was a foreign concept.

Before Lucifer became evil, he was the top worshiper of God. It wasn't until he became aware that he was getting a lot of attention from other angels that he began to feel himself a little too much. Then he felt as if he could do what God could and he began desiring to be God. With his popularity with the angels, his reputation was built up and spread all over the heavens with the other angels making Lucifer's ego impossible to shut down. His weapon to win the angels' hearts was entertainment. He used that to get them to trust in him. He displayed a talent and beauty they couldn't resist.

The angels lost sight of the real and true Creator because God did not make a display of Himself, flaunting what He could do. Instead, He simply was. His very being should have spoken to them, but they were drawn away by Lucifer's display of what he could do. They should have looked around at the Heavens and been reminded of the creative power of God. They should have recognized the joy and peace of His presence and the fulfillment of purpose as displays of God's power, but they did not. We too are drawn away by displays and distractions. We forget the power and joy and peace of God, especially when we are facing trials or struggling with life. That's why a firm foundation is important.

The devil is the total opposite of God. He has to show out and make a scene. That's why at the end, before Heaven was cleaned out from evil, more angels trusted the devil because of what they saw over what they had always known. That was the beginning of their own destruction. They trusted in the idea of someone being god instead of the true and living God. They knew that Lucifer was an angel just like them but because of his reputation they believed he could become much more.

Spirit realm:

God is real! Angels are real! The devil and his demons are real! Just because we cannot physically see into the spirit realm does not mean it does not exist. The spirit realm is real, even more real than us. One way of understanding the spirit realm is understanding this: "What's dead can live! What lives can die!" I guess that's the best way to describe it, meaning, angels, unlike us, were brought into the spirit realm full of life, no darkness. But once they were tested, they too died spiritually. But we are the opposite. We are born alive but also born with a sinful nature. Sin leads to spiritual death. We are spiritually dead until we accept Jesus into our lives and repent of our sin. Then we become alive spiritually. When we die physically, our bodies are dead, but our spirits are alive with Christ. By believing in Jesus and confessing our sin we gain that new life

A simple way to put it is that the spirit realm is made up of good and evil. There is no in between. But "good" is too simple of a word. A better way to describe it is righteousness and evil. God and His angels are good and dwell in Heaven where righteousness abounds. The devil and his demons are evil and dwell in Hell where unrighteousness abounds. This good and evil, righteousness and unrighteousness spills over onto earth. The flesh fights the spirit just like good fights evil.

Something important to know about the spirit realm is that the devil is not after just anyone. He purposefully and specifically goes after God's anointed, the ones he feels are a threat to his kingdom. That's right. Satan believes he is building a kingdom, the kingdom of darkness but in reality, he is only building what will be destroyed. With no firm foundation and no creative gift, he just builds and builds and builds that which will crumble.

Everyone else is an easy target for the demons to contain because they are already living their lives outside of God's plan and purpose. The devil moves when he feels the need to stop God's kingdom from taking over. Spiritually powerful people attract the devil because he wants to prove a point to God that he is better because he stole them. Once again, it is all about his pride. It is all about his desire to be worshipped instead of God. Though the devil continues to plot and scheme, he has not changed. His tactics and motives are the same since he first rebelled against God. Seeking out people who are following after God and sharing the life changing message of the Gospel is his main goal. He seeks to bring confusion and doubt and resentment and to deposit his pride into the lives of believers. Again, this is why believers must be strong in the Lord, they must put on the full armor of God as Ephesians 6 states, "Finally, be strong in the Lord and in his mighty power. Put on the full armor of God, so that you can take your stand against the devil's schemes. For our struggle is not against flesh and blood, but against the rulers, against the authorities, against the powers of this dark world and against the spiritual forces of evil in the heavenly realms. Therefore, put on the full armor of God, so that when the day of evil comes, you may be able to stand your ground, and after you have done everything, to stand. Stand firm then, with the belt of truth buckled around your waist, with the breastplate of righteousness in place, and with your feet fitted with the readiness that comes from the gospel of peace. In addition to all this, take up the shield of faith, with which you can extinguish all the flaming arrows of the evil one. Take the helmet of salvation and the sword of the Spirit, which is the word of God. And pray in the Spirit on all occasions with all kinds of prayers and requests. With this in mind, be alert and always keep on praying for all the Lord's people."

Here are some words of wisdom about God! God Himself cannot be figured out. No one can predict what He will or will not do. He's very spontaneous. He just does different things at different times when you least expect it. That's what I love about Him. He catches you off guard and it's always the perfect time. What we can be sure about is His character. He will never operate outside of His nature. We can be assured of this. The Bible tells us that He is God, and He will not change. Though we may not know how or when He will act or move, we can know that He will move in love because God is love. God is all about love and He interacts with us as our Father. Just as with an earthly father, God will not do all the work for us, but He will point us in the right direction. God is all about us growing and developing daily. He equips us with what we need to get through daily challenges. No handouts are given. He wants us to work no matter who we are. God is very serious and straight to the point. No joke! He gets straight to the point. "Hot or cold" No in between. He is a jealous God! Don't ever put any-thing or anyone before Him because He will let it be known. He's hard working. I know most may think He's sitting back enjoying it. Not yet, He's hard at work getting heaven and earth the way He intended in The Beginning

CPSIA information can be obtained
at www.ICGtesting.com
Printed in the USA
BVHW081431030522
635996BV00031B/2220